DID YOU KNOW? BUGS

20 THINGS YOU DIDN'T KNOW ABOUT PRAYING MANTISES

DOUG BRADLEY

PowerKiDS press

Published in 2027 by The Rosen Publishing Group, Inc.
2544 Clinton Street, Buffalo, NY 14224

Portions of this work were originally authored by Adrienne Houk Maley and published as *20 Fun Facts About Praying Mantises*. All new material in this edition was authored by Doug Bradley.

Editor: Greg Roza
Book Design: Michael Flynn

Photo Credits: Cover Marinodenisenko/Shutterstock.com; series background freshcare/Shutterstock.com; p. 4 Uros Poteko/Alamy; p. 5 blickwinkel/F. Teigler/Alamy; p. 6 imageBROKER/Reinhard Hoelzl/Alamy; p. 7 Simon Kovacic/Alamy; p. 8 Christoph Bosch/Alamy; p. 9 Juanma Aparicio/Alamy; pp. 10–11 Michael Wesemann/Alamy; p. 12 Goran Šafarek/Alamy; p. 13 Macky Albor/Alamy; p. 14 dwi putra/Alamy; p. 15 Image Professionals GmbH/TravelCollection/Alamy; p. 16 piemags/nature/Alamy; p. 17 ephotocorp/Sagar Khunte/Alamy; p. 18 Daniel Borzynski/Alamy; p. 19 Razvan Cornel Constantin/Alamy; p. 20 Heckepics/Alamy; p. 21 Mertiny, A./Juniors@wildlife/Alamy; p. 22 Aliaksei Smalenski/Alamy; p. 23 Premaphotos/Alamy; p. 24 Goran Šafarek/Alamy; p. 25 Nature Picture Library/ Jose B. Ruiz/Alamy; p. 26 Jure Simunic/Alamy; p. 27 EDU Vision/Alamy; p. 29 Mint Images Limited/Alamy.

Cataloging-in-Publication Data

Names: Bradley, Doug, 1971-.
Title: 20 things you didn't know about praying mantises / Doug Bradley.
Description: Buffalo, New York : PowerKids Press, 2027. | Series: Did you know? bugs | Includes glossary and index.
Identifiers: ISBN 9781499457421 (pbk.) | ISBN 9781499457438 (library bound) | ISBN 9781499457445 (ebook)
Subjects: LCSH: Praying mantis–Juvenile literature.
Classification: LCC QL505.9 B656 2027 | DDC 595.727–dc2

Printed in China

CPSIA Compliance Information: Batch #QSPK27. For Further Information contact Rosen Publishing at 1-800-237-9932.

CONTENTS

ALIEN BUGS?

Praying mantises are strange-looking bugs! They almost look like aliens with their long, jointed legs and large head. They can be hard to find because they blend in so well with their surroundings.

Many people think praying mantises look as if they're praying, which is where the name comes from. Some people think they look like they're about to do kung fu! Maybe that's why other bugs stay far away. Praying mantises are capable hunters that many animals try to avoid.

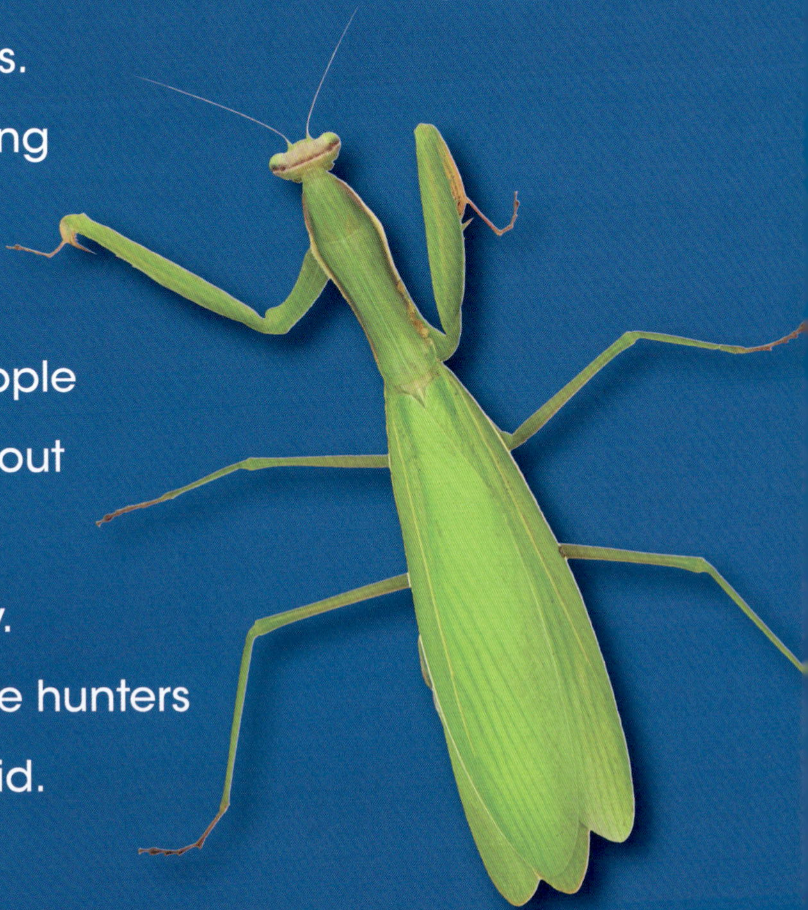

There are many species, or kinds, of praying mantises. Depending on the species, an adult praying mantis can be 0.5 to 6 inches (1.3 to 15.2 cm) long.

BODY PARTS

FACT 1

A PRAYING MANTIS'S FRONT LEGS CAN STRIKE A TARGET IN 1/20 OF A SECOND.

The praying mantis's front legs are like spring-loaded weapons! Most **prey** never see them coming. These strong, spiny legs can easily hold on to struggling prey. A praying mantis can easily crush a grasshopper or cricket with its front legs.

Once a praying mantis snatches its prey in its forelegs it quickly eats it alive.

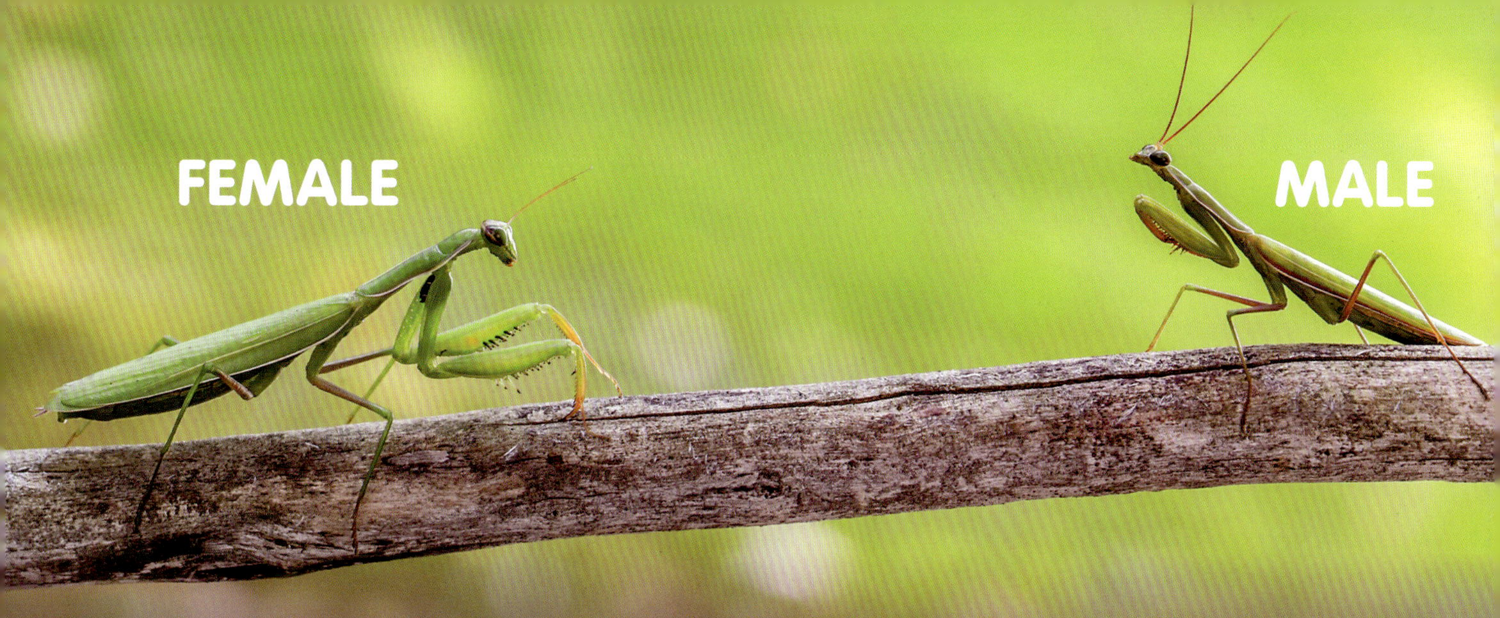

A female mantis has a longer, heavier body than a male.

PRAYING MANTISES HAVE WINGS, BUT MOST FEMALE PRAYING MANTISES CAN'T FLY.

FACT 2

Mantises have two sets of wings. The two larger outer wings protect the two smaller inner wings. A male's wings are longer than a female's wings. Males can fly short distances to get away from **predators**. Female mantises are heavier. They jump and crawl, but they usually can't fly.

FACT 3

THE PRAYING MANTIS CAN TURN ITS HEAD 180 DEGREES, OR HALFWAY AROUND.

The praying mantis is **flexible**! This is an **adaptation** that helps the praying mantis locate and follow its prey. Just before it attacks, it sways its body back and forth. Swaying may help a praying mantis judge how far it needs to jump to get its prey.

Swaying also helps a praying mantis hide among leaves moving in the wind.

A PRAYING MANTIS ISN'T PRAYING. IT'S WAITING FOR A MEAL TO PASS BY.

FACT 4

The praying mantis's large, bent front legs look like a person praying. However, these legs are just waiting to spring out and grab a meal. The forelegs have spines to help hold wiggling prey in place. This is an example of an animal **ambushing** its prey.

MANTIS PARTS

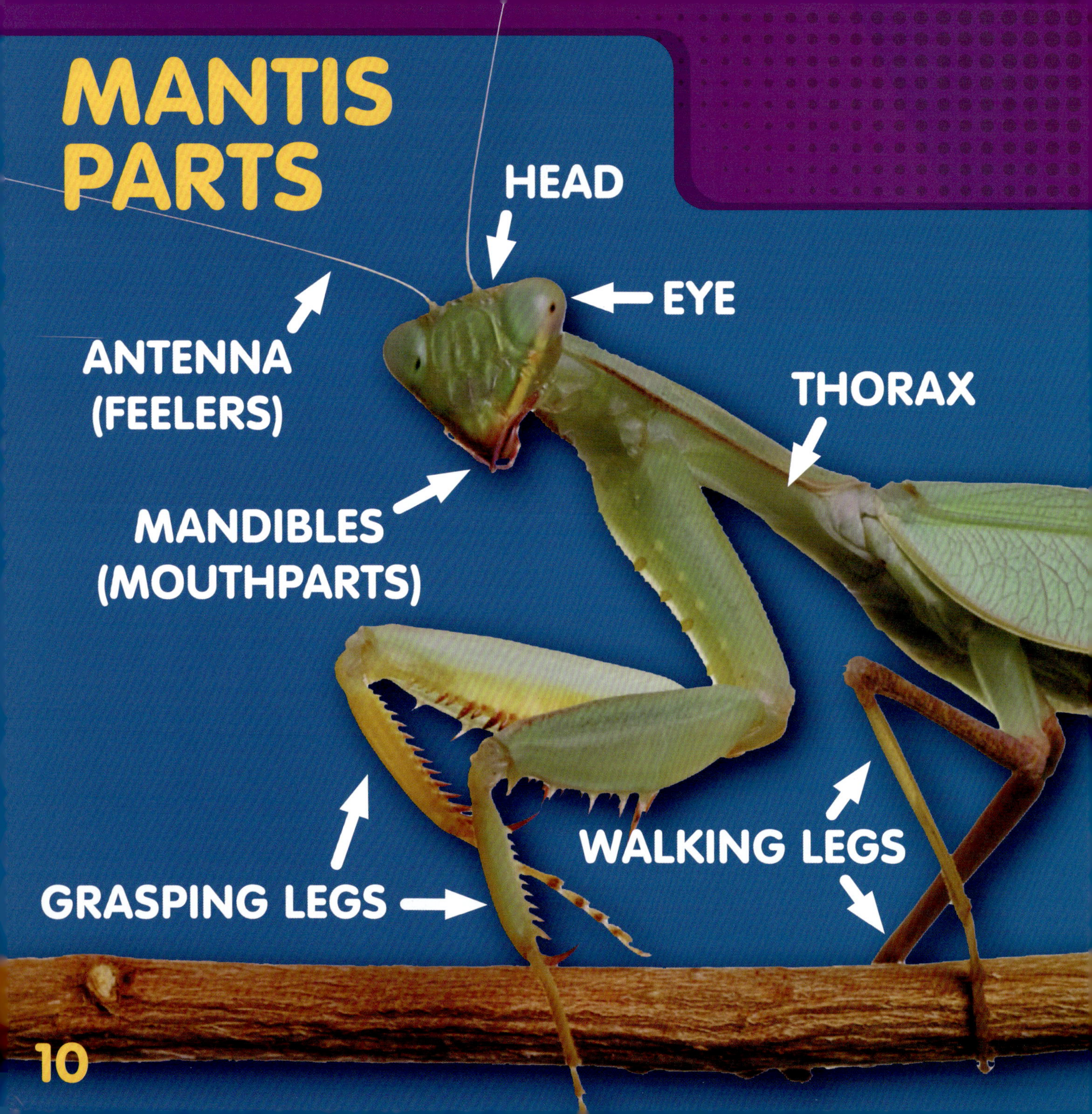

ABDOMEN
WALKING LEGS

MANTIS EYES

FACT 5

PRAYING MANTISES HAVE SUPERIOR VISION.

Praying mantises can detect quick movements and see objects as far as 50 feet (15 m) away. Their large eyes are **compound eyes**. Flies have compound eyes, too, but many can only see objects clearly a few millimeters away.

The compound eye of the praying mantis has thousands of light-sensitive parts. Each one is like a tiny eye that processes visual information.

Praying mantises can see nearly all the way around them. This makes it hard to sneak up on them.

PRAYING MANTISES HAVE TWO KINDS OF EYES.

FACT 6

A praying mantis's compound eyes are on the sides of its triangular-shaped head. They're very good at seeing everything around them, especially movement. Praying mantises also have three simple eyes between their two large eyes. These smaller eyes, called ocelli, can only sense light.

MANTIS HEARING

FACT 7

A PRAYING MANTIS'S EAR IS ON THE MIDDLE OF ITS BODY.

The praying mantis has an ear on its **abdomen**. This ear helps the praying mantis detect sound waves that bats use to catch prey. When it hears the sounds, the praying mantis dives out of the way of the hungry bat.

A praying mantis's abdomen contains several important organs, including those that allow them to breathe and digest, or break down, food.

Bats are a major predator of praying mantises. Other mantis predators include birds, spiders, frogs, and lizards.

THE PRAYING MANTIS'S EXCELLENT HEARING ALLOWS IT TO DODGE BAT ATTACKS.

FACT 8

Once the praying mantis hears a bat, it gets out of the way by opening its wings and diving down. Scientists have found that the louder a bat's signal, the more moves the praying mantis makes while fleeing.

SO MANY SPECIES

FACT 9

MORE THAN 2,000 SPECIES OF MANTISES LIVE ALL OVER THE WORLD.

Praying mantises can be found in many warm regions around the world. They're also found in cooler parts of North America and Europe. The California mantis is the only species that's native to the United States.

California mantises can be 2 to 5 inches (5 to 12 cm) long.

PRAYING MANTISES AND COCKROACHES ARE CLOSE COUSINS.

FACT 10

Mantises and cockroaches are both are part of the Dictyoptera (dihk-tee-AHP-tuh-ruh) order of insects. This word comes from the ancient Greek words for "net" and "wing." Mantises and cockroaches both have leathery wings and chewing mouthparts.

LET'S EAT!

FACT 11

PRAYING MANTISES EAT QUICKLY, OFTEN LEAVING JUST A FEW LIMBS BEHIND.

Many kinds of insects, such as mosquitoes, butterflies, and honeybees, have mouthparts that suck up food. Not praying mantises. They move their jaws sideways to chew live prey. Mantis jaws are called mandibles.

This mantis is eating a honeybee.

The size and lightning-quick speed of a praying mantis helps it capture all sorts of prey.

PRAYING MANTISES SOMETIMES KILL AND EAT LARGER ANIMALS.

FACT 12

Praying mantises aren't picky eaters. They eat almost any kind of insect. These predators creep up slowly on prey and then ambush them. They sometimes hunt small mice, frogs, lizards, hummingbirds, and even snakes.

GET A GOOD LOOK

FACT 13

PRAYING MANTISES CAN HIDE IN PLAIN SIGHT.

Mantises are masters of **camouflage**! Green meadows are a great place for green praying mantises to hide. The damper the air is, the greener the mantis will appear. The ghost mantis looks like a dried-up leaf. The orchid mantis has legs that look like pink flowers.

The ghost mantis looks like a dried-up leaf. Most predators don't even notice it.

This praying mantis uses its legs to make it look like it has two huge eyes!

ONCE A PREDATOR SPOTS A PRAYING MANTIS, THE MANTIS WILL MAKE ITSELF LOOK LARGER AND SCARIER.

FACT 14

When a praying mantis is in trouble, it may stand tall and spread out its wings. Some have brightly colored wings that tell enemies to stay away. They also make hissing sounds, open their mouths, and grab with their front legs.

GROWING UP

FACT 15

FEMALE PRAYING MANTISES LAY BETWEEN 10 TO 400 EGGS AT ONE TIME, DEPENDING ON THE SPECIES.

In fall, female praying mantises lay eggs close to the ground. They surround the eggs with a foamy substance that hardens to forms cases called oothecae (oh-uh-THEE-kee). They're almost impossible to find. This protects the many tiny praying mantises, called nymphs, growing inside.

Oothecae are strong enough to last the winter. Here, tiny praying mantises emerge from a egg case in spring.

These mantis nymphs haven't grown wings yet.

BABY PRAYING MANTISES LOOK LIKE SMALL COPIES OF ADULT MANTISES.

FACT 16

Baby mantis nymphs get their good looks from their parents! Nymphs all emerge from the egg case at about the same time. Nymphs don't have wings yet, but will grow them when they reach adulthood.

FACT 17

PRAYING MANTISES SHED THEIR OUTER COVERING SIX TO NINE TIMES BEFORE REACHING ADULT SIZE.

Praying mantises molt, or shed their **exoskeleton**, several times as they grow larger. Once it gets too big for its outer skin, it stretches, splits its skin, and slowly wiggles out of it. The mantis hangs upside down while its new exoskeleton hardens.

Praying mantises molt every 9 to 15 days.

HEADS UP!

FACT 18

FEMALE PRAYING MANTISES HAVE BEEN KNOWN TO EAT THE HEAD OF THEIR MATE!

Female praying mantises may eat some or all of their mate's head while **mating**. Scientists aren't sure why. They might need the **nutrients** for their young. When approaching a female, males often approach them from behind to avoid being eaten!

Some scientists think **captive** females become angry, causing them to eat their mates. It doesn't happen as often in the wild.

IN THE GARDEN

FACT 19

PRAYING MANTISES ARE GREAT GARDENERS.

Praying mantises are great for garden pest control. They'll eat just about any insect. If you see one in the garden, leave it alone so it can protect your plants by eating harmful pests, such as grasshoppers and beetles.

You can order oothecae online and receive them in the mail! By placing the egg case in your garden in spring, praying mantises will help keep your garden free of pests.

PRAYING MANTISES ARE CANNIBALS!

FACT 20

Unfortunately, it can be hard to keep praying mantises in a garden because they're cannibalistic. That means they eat each other! If you want more mantises in the garden, avoid using pesticides, which are substances used to kill bugs.

EARTHLY BUGS

Only 20 kinds of praying mantises live in North America, while Africa has 880 known species. That's because mantises prefer to live in warmer climates. If you're lucky enough to come across a praying mantis, take the time to observe its weird body features and habits.

Do you think praying mantises look like aliens from another world? Now you know that they're more at home in gardens than outer space! They blend in with their surroundings so well that they're hard to see no matter where in the world you are.

Praying mantises can be kept as pets as long as you feed them live food, usually lots of crickets.

GLOSSARY

abdomen: The part of an insect's body that contains the stomach.

adaptation: A change in a type of animal that happens over time and makes it better able to live in its surroundings.

alien: A living thing not from Earth.

ambush: To attack from a hiding place.

camouflage: Colors or shapes on animals that allow them to blend in with their surroundings.

captive: The state of being caged.

compound eye: An eye made up of many separate seeing parts.

exoskeleton: The hard outer covering of an animal's body.

flexible: Able to bend easily.

mate: To come together to make babies. Also, one of two animals that come together to produce babies.

nutrient: Something a living thing needs to grow and stay alive.

predator: An animal that hunts other animals for food.

prey: An animal that is hunted by other animals for food.

FOR MORE INFORMATION

BOOKS

Downs, Kieran. *Praying Mantis vs. Black Widow Spider.* Minnetonka, MN: Torque, 2022.

Rose, Rachel. *Praying Mantises.* Bloomington, MN: Bearport Publishing, 2025.

WEBSITES

A Comprehensive Guide to Keeping Praying Mantises
vetverified.com/articles/a-comprehensive-guide-to-keeping-praying-mantises
Want to know what it takes to raise your own praying mantises? This site has the answers!

The Praying Mantis
www.theprayingmantis.org
Learn much more about praying mantises on this site dedicated to the insect.

Publisher's note to educators and parents: Our editors have carefully reviewed these websites to ensure that they are suitable for students. Many websites change frequently, however, and we cannot guarantee that a site's future contents will continue to meet our high standards of quality and educational value. Be advised that students should be closely supervised whenever they access the internet.

INDEX